cooking the CHINESE way

Spiced roast chicken is served on a bed of green lettuce. (Recipe on page 34.)

cooking the
CHINESE way

LING YU

easy menu
ethnic
cookbooks

Lerner Publications Company ■ Minneapolis

Series Editor: Patricia A. Grotts

Series Consultant: Ann L. Burckhardt

Drawings and Map by Jeanette Swofford

The page border for this book is based on the Chinese lotus flower symbol. The lotus flower, symbolizing summer and fruitfulness, was sacred to the people of ancient China.

Pinyin spelling is used for the names of the cities and other geographical locations shown on the map. (The more conventional spellings appear in parentheses following the pinyin spellings.) The pinyin system uses the 26-letter Roman alphabet in the way that best recreates the sounds of Mandarin Chinese. It was adopted by mainland China (but not Taiwan) in 1978, and China has requested that all Chinese words and names appearing in English and other foreign language publications be written in pinyin.

This book is dedicated with love to the children of the world

Copyright © 1982 by Lerner Publications Company

Library of Congress Cataloging in Publication Data

Yu, Ling.
   Cooking the Chinese way.

   (Easy menu ethnic cookbooks)
   Includes index.
   Summary: Introduces fundamentals of Chinese cooking, including special ingredients and cooking utensils. Also provides recipes for suggested dishes.
     1. Cookery, Chinese—Juvenile literature.
   2. China—Juvenile literature. |1. Cookery, Chinese.
   2. China—Social life and customs| I. Title.
   II. Series.
   TX724.5.C5Y74   641.5951   82-263
   ISBN 0-8225-0902-4   AACR2

Manufactured in the United States of America

1 2 3 4 5 6 7 8 9 10 91 90 89 88 87 86 85 84 83 82

CONTENTS

Amur (Amur River)

Tai Hanggan Ling
(Greater Khingan Range)

Xiao Hanggan Ling
(Lesser Khingan Range)

Fruit

Liao He (Liao River)

Changbai Shan
(Ch'ang Pai Mountains)

Altay Shan
(Altai Mountains)

Tian Shan
(Tien Shan Mountains)

Pamir Shan
(Pamir Mountains)

Beijing Area

● **Beijing** (Peking)

Cows

Vegetables

CHINA

Huang Hai
(Yellow Sea)

Kunlun Shan
(Kunlun Mountains)

Huang He (Huang Ho River)

Grain

Chang Jiang (Yangtze River)

Himalaya Shan
(Himalaya Mountains)

Qin Ling
(Tsinling Mountains)

Nanjing
(Nanking)

● **Shanghai**

Forest
Products

Sichuan Area
(Szechuan Area)

Shanghai
Area

Mt. Everest

Leeks,
Garlic,
Onions

Chang Jiang (Yangtze River)

Hogs

Poultry

Dong Hai
(East China Sea)

Tea

Guangdong
(Canton Area)

Taiwan
(Republic
of China)

Xi Jiang (Hsi Chiang River)

● **Guangzhou** (Canton)

Rice

Xiang Gang
(Hong Kong)

Hainan

Nan Hai
(South China Sea)

Seafood

INTRODUCTION

Despite the fact that people in many Western countries enjoy eating Chinese cuisine, preparing Chinese food at home is still unfamiliar to most Western cooks. Actually, there is nothing mysterious about basic Chinese cooking. It is simple, economical, and nutritious, as well as tasty. Perhaps the easiest way to understand Chinese cooking is to learn a little about the background of China and its people.

THE LAND

China is the oldest continuing civilization in the world. Its sophisticated art, literature, philosophy, religion, and cuisine have been developed over thousands of years. Basic to the character of the Chinese people is their relationship to the land. Farming has always been their chief occupation. Archaeologists have uncovered farming tools and pots containing grains of rice that date back to 5000 B.C. Such finds indicate that agriculture was an important part of ancient Chinese society, just as it is today.

China's farmers, however, have not always been prosperous. This is partly due to the size of China's population. One-fifth of all the people in the world live in China. China is not much larger than the United States in area, yet it has a population of more than 950 million—four times that of the United States.

In this vast country, only 13 percent of the land can be cultivated. Thus, food has been scarce throughout China's history. With such a large population to feed and so little farming and grazing land, the Chinese have always placed a high value on food. They seldom waste anything. Since many workers are needed to tend the land, Chinese farm families have traditionally been large and close-knit.

Stretching the food budget without sacrificing nutrition and enjoyment is a daily challenge. Meat, which is a luxury, is cut into small pieces. Vegetables are added to increase the size of the servings. Rice or noodles are a basic part of every meal and provide a cheap way to fill empty stomachs.

COOKING TECHNIQUES

Through the centuries, Chinese cooking has also adapted itself to an ever-present shortage of fuel. Because wood and other fuels for cooking have always been scarce, the Chinese have learned to spend a maximum amount of time in food preparation and a minimum of time in actual cooking.

Most ingredients are diced, sliced, or shredded because small-sized pieces cook faster. The seasonings are measured out ahead of time. Most cooking is done in one pot and usually takes only a few minutes.

One quick-cooking technique is the *stir-fry* method in which meats, fish, or vegetables are cut into small pieces and tossed rapidly in hot oil. This method has been developed to insure that the nutritional value, flavor, and color of foods are not lost during cooking. *Steaming* food is another quick method of cooking that preserves flavor and food value.

REGIONS OF CHINA

Because they have had to use every available food source, Chinese cooks have learned to cook a wide variety of unusual foods. It has been said that the Chinese can find a way to cook anything!

Often, the ingredients used in Chinese dishes reflect the regions from which the dishes come. Over the centuries, each area of China has developed its own distinct dialect, customs, and character. Because climate and, consequently, available foods vary from region to region in this large country, each section has its own unique kind of cooking. Although basic cooking techniques are the same all over China, each region features special ingredients and seasonings. In general, there are four main "schools" of Chinese cooking, each from a particular part of China.

Cantonese cooking is associated with the city of Canton (Guangzhou) and southern China. Most of the Chinese who emigrated to Western countries during the 19th century came from Canton, and for this reason

Cantonese food is the most familiar to Westerners. Sweet and sour pork and wonton soup, for example, come from Canton.

Cantonese dishes are usually stir-fried and lightly seasoned. Rice is the staple food of this region.

The *Peking (Beijing)* or *Mandarin* style of cooking developed in northern China. Here the staple food is not rice but wheat flour. The flour is made into noodles, steamed bread, and dumplings. The most famous delicacy of this region is Peking duck.

Ginger root, scallions, soy sauce, bean sprouts, cabbage, and hoisin sauce are all used in Chinese cooking.

On the eastern coast, *Shanghai* cooking dominates. The dishes are strongly flavored with soy sauce and sugar and include a wide range of readily available seafood. On the whole, the food is rich and tangy because of the sauces used.

In inland China, the *Szechuan (Sichuan)* style of cooking (si-CHWAN) produces hot, spicy dishes. This style of cuisine contains a great deal of hot pepper, garlic, onions, and leeks.

As you can see, Chinese cooking is varied, nutritious, and highly adaptable. Best of all, it can be prepared by anyone. The recipes selected for this book are simple and require few ingredients.

Once you, as a beginner, have learned the main principles and a few basic recipes, you may go on to make elaborate dishes or to create some variations of your own. This is an opportunity to be creative, and your efforts will have a practical result—something good to eat!

BEFORE YOU BEGIN

Cooking any dish, plain or fancy, is easier and more fun if you are familiar with its ingredients. Chinese cooking makes use of some ingredients that are not well known to Westerners. Sometimes special cookware is used, too, although the recipes in this book can easily be prepared with ordinary utensils and pans.

Before you start cooking, carefully study the following "dictionary" of special ingredients, terms, and utensils. Then read through the recipe you want to try from beginning to end. Now you are ready to shop for ingredients and to organize the cookware you will need. Once you have assembled everything, you can begin to cook. It is also very important to read *The Careful Cook* on page 42. Following these rules will make your cooking experience safe, fun, and easy.

COOKING UTENSILS

cleaver—The Chinese use a cleaver to cut, slice, chop, shred, and section foods. An all-purpose knife works just as well.

spatula—The curved Chinese spatula is used to toss, turn, and scoop up food, usually during stir-frying. Any kind of wooden or metal spatula can be used.

wok—The wok has been used to cook one-dish meals in Chinese homes for centuries. It is an all-purpose pot used for deep-frying, stir-frying, and steaming. Made of steel, aluminum, or cast iron, it has a rounded bottom and sloping sides. It is held upright by a collar-like stand or ring. A large skillet or an electric frying pan can be easily substituted for a wok.

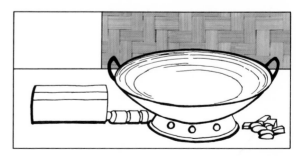

The cleaver and the wok are traditional Chinese utensils. Use the cleaver to chop up the food to be cooked in your wok.

COOKING TERMS

boil—To heat a liquid over high heat until bubbles form and rise rapidly to the surface

brown—To cook food quickly in fat over high heat so that the surface turns an even brown

cut in—A way to combine solid fat and flour using your fingers, a pastry blender, or two knives. Cut or break fat into small pieces and mix them throughout the flour until mixture has a coarse, mealy consistency.

deep fry—To cook food by immersing it completely in very hot fat or oil. This cooking method seals in flavor and gives food a crispy surface.

marinate—To soak food in a liquid in order to add flavor and to tenderize it

mince—To chop food into very small pieces

preheat—To allow an oven to warm up to a certain temperature before putting food in it

roast—To cook in an open pan in an oven so that heat penetrates the food from all sides

Shrimp and peas are ideal foods for stir-frying in a wok. Use a curved Chinese spatula to toss, turn, and scoop up food for serving.

simmer—To cook over low heat in liquid kept just below its boiling point. Bubbles may occasionally rise to the surface.

stir-fry—To cook meat, vegetables, poultry, or fish in a small amount of vegetable oil over high heat, stirring constantly. All ingredients are cut into small pieces before stir-frying so that they will cook rapidly. Because of quick cooking, meats are firm yet tender, and vegetables stay fresh and crunchy.

SPECIAL INGREDIENTS

almond extract—A liquid made from the oil of the almond nut that is used to give an almond flavor to food

bamboo shoots—Tender, fleshy yellow sprouts from bamboo canes. They can be bought fresh or canned whole or thinly sliced.

bean sprouts—Sprouts from the Mung bean that can be bought either canned or fresh. These crunchy white vegetables can be eaten raw or mixed with other ingredients in stir-fried dishes. (Be sure not to confuse bean sprouts with alfalfa sprouts, which are smaller and finer.)

chard—A vegetable with dark green, yellow, or bright red leaves. Its stalks and leaves can be cooked or eaten raw.

Chinese or celery cabbage—A pale green vegetable with broad, tightly packed leaves. It is often used in soup and stir-fried dishes. (Any other leafy green vegetable, such as fresh spinach or chard, can be substituted for Chinese cabbage.)

cornstarch—A fine white starch made from corn, commonly used for thickening sauces and gravies. *(When you use cornstarch in a recipe, put the required amount of dry cornstarch in a cup and add just enough cold water to form a smooth, thin paste. Then add to the other ingredients. This method keeps the cornstarch from forming lumps when cooked in liquid.)*

duck or plum sauce—A thick sauce often used as a dip for appetizers. It is made from plums, chilies, sugar, and spices.

garlic—An herb whose distinctive flavor is used in many dishes. Fresh garlic can usually be found in the produce department of a supermarket. Each piece of bulb can be broken up into several small sections called cloves. Most recipes use only one or two finely chopped cloves of this very strong herb. Before you chop up a clove of garlic, you will have to remove the brittle, papery covering that surrounds it.

gelatin—A clear, powdered protein substance used as a thickening agent

ginger root—A knobby, light brown root used to flavor food. To use fresh ginger root, slice or grate off the amount called for and freeze the rest. Fresh ginger has a very zippy taste, so use it sparingly. (Don't substitute dried ground ginger in a recipe calling for fresh ginger as the taste is very different.)

hoisin sauce—A dark, sweet, thick sauce made from soybeans, sugar, and spices. It can be used in cooking or as a dip.

oyster sauce—A sauce made from oysters, sugar, and soy sauce. It is sometimes used in place of soy sauce in cooking and also as a dip.

rice—There are three main varieties of rice. *Long-grain rice,* the kind used in the recipes in this book, is fluffy and absorbs more water than other types. *Short-grain rice* has shorter, thicker grains which tend to stick together when cooked. *Sweet or glutinous rice* is used only for making Chinese pastries and special festival dishes.

scallions—Another name for green onions

sesame oil—An oil made from sesame seeds. Since it has a strong flavor, only a few drops are needed in most dishes.

soy sauce—A sauce made from soybeans that is used as a salt substitute in Chinese cooking. Light soy sauces are saltier than the dark ones.

sugar or snow peas—Tender, green pea pods that can be bought fresh or frozen

water chestnuts—Sweet, crisp root vegetables that are widely used in salads, soups, sauces, and as a garnish

watercress—A green plant with broad leaves that has a peppery flavor. It is used in salads, soups, sauces, and as a garnish.

wonton skins—Small, thin squares of soft dough made from flour, water, and eggs. They can be bought frozen or refrigerated.

Worcestershire sauce—A commercially prepared sauce made from vinegar, soy sauce, spices, molasses, garlic, chilies, and green onion

A CHINESE TABLE

The Chinese way of serving food evolved on the farms, where families were large and close-knit. Eating together with members of the family or close friends was, and still is, a great pleasure in China. Chinese family meals are served communal style. The food is put on large platters and placed in the center of a round table so everybody can reach all the dishes easily. Each diner takes what he or she wants from each platter and fills his or her own bowl.

Place settings are simple. To set a typical Chinese table you need the following items for each person:

a pair of chopsticks and a soup bowl
a porcelain soup spoon
a rice bowl and saucer
a tiny saucer for bones

With communal platters of food and such simple place settings, unexpected guests at dinner time can be easily accommodated. As the Chinese say, you need only add a bowl and a pair of chopsticks.

EATING WITH CHOPSTICKS

To Westerners, chopsticks are usually the most exotic item on the list of serving utensils. But chopsticks are not difficult to manage once you have learned the basic technique. The key to using them is to hold the inside stick still while moving the outside stick back and forth. The pair then acts as pincers to pick up pieces of food.

Hold the thicker end of the first chopstick in the crook of your thumb, resting the lower part lightly against the inside of your ring finger.

Then put the second chopstick between the tips of your index and middle fingers and hold it with your thumb, much as you would hold a pencil.

Now you can make the outer chopstick move by bending your index and middle fingers toward the inside chopstick. The tips of the two sticks should come together like pincers when you bend your fingers. Once you get a feel for the technique, just keep practicing. Soon you'll be an expert!

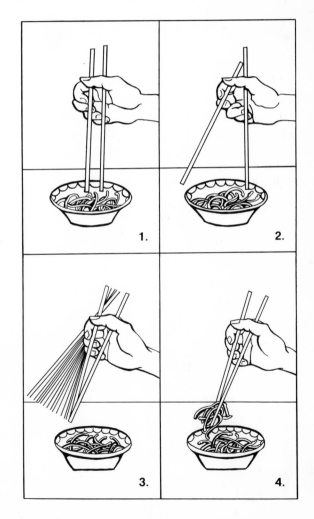

A CHINESE MENU

In China, a meal features a succession of main dishes, each of which are equally important. The flavors and textures in each dish must harmonize with one another, yet provide variety.

An informal family meal usually includes a light soup, a meat dish, a fish dish, and a vegetable dish. The foundation of the meal is rice or noodles of some kind. Fresh fruits are usually served for dessert instead of sweets.

For a feast or dinner party, the menu may include 12 or more dishes, each of which is served as a separate course. A feast may begin with appetizers and then move through a succession of hot dishes—chicken, fish, shellfish, beef, pork, egg, bean curd, and vegetables—and several soups. Rice or noodles and sometimes a sweet dessert are also included.

The following are simplified menu plans for two family meals and a dinner party. There are no specific recipes for a Chinese breakfast or lunch in this book because the Chinese do not have many dishes that are served only for those meals. Rice, vegetables, fish, and meat are eaten at any time of the day and are combined in many different ways. The combinations of dishes given are only suggestions. It is fun to experiment and discover the menu plans that you like best.

FAMILY MEALS

Watercress soup
Stir-fried beef with sugar peas *or* Spiced
    roast chicken
Bean sprouts with scallions
Plain rice   Tea
Fruit *or* Fortune cookies

Wonton soup
Pork with green pepper and pineapple *or*
    Fried rice with ham
Chinese cabbage
Plain rice   Tea
Almond cookies

DINNER PARTY

Wonton
Egg-flower chicken soup
Cantonese-style barbecued spareribs
Shrimp with hoisin sauce
Savory beef stew
Chinese cabbage
Plain rice   Tea
Almond fruit float

Left: Soup, rice, and a simple stir-fry dish of beef with sugar peas (recipe on page 29) make up a typical family meal. *Right:* Shrimp with hoisin sauce (recipe on page 35) is one of several courses that could be served at a Chinese dinner party.

Serve hot fragrant tea from a pretty Chinese teapot.

CHINESE BASICS

Tea

The Chinese have been drinking tea for centuries. Tea is an integral part of the Chinese way of life and is drunk every-where in China at all times of the day and evening.

There are many kinds of Chinese tea, but generally they can be divided into three kinds—green, black, and oolong. Green teas are mild in flavor. Jasmine, the most well known, has a delicate, flowerlike taste and aroma. The black teas have a stronger taste. Oolong is a pale brown tea with a distinctive flavor often compared to that of fresh peaches.

Chinese tea usually comes in loose form rather than in tea bags. It is drunk plain; sugar, lemon, or cream are never added. The following method of preparing tea will give the best results.

1. In a teakettle or saucepan, bring water to a boil.
2. Take a teapot (earthenware or china is better than metal), and rinse with boiling water.
3. Measure loose tea into the pot. You may use 1 teaspoon of tea for each cup of water, but the exact amount is really up to your own taste. (You'll probably have to experiment a little to brew it just the way you like it.)
4. Pour boiling water into the teapot to make the right amount of tea according to the strength you like.
5. Cover the teapot and let stand for a few minutes.
6. Pour tea directly into cups.

Rice is nutritious, inexpensive, and very easy to prepare. It is delicious to eat either by itself or with other dishes.

Rice

Rice is the basic food of the Chinese people. In China, people eat rice three times a day. Plain rice can be a part of any meal. Any leftovers can be used to make fried rice (see page 26), so you will seldom have to waste this versatile food.

**2 cups long-grain rice, uncooked
3 cups water**

1. Put rice and water in a deep saucepan. Do not cover.
2. Put the pan over high heat and bring water to a boil.
3. Turn the heat down to medium and cook rice for 10 minutes.
4. Lower the heat and cover the pan.
5. Simmer rice for 20 minutes or until all water has been absorbed.

Serves 4

APPETIZERS

The Chinese word for appetizer is *dim sum,* which means "touch of heart." In China, these tidbits of food are not always eaten before a meal as appetizers are in the West. Instead, they are usually served with tea as mid-morning, afternoon, or late-night snacks. Typical snacks are egg rolls, fried wonton, shrimp balls, and filled dumplings.

The appetizers shown above include filled dump-lings, egg rolls, and wonton.

Wonton

These tasty meat-filled bundles may be fried and eaten as appetizers or boiled and added to soup. The literal English translation of the word "wonton" is "swallowing a cloud." If you take a close look at wonton soup, you will see that the wonton do resemble white, puffy clouds, floating across the sky!

½ **pound ground pork or beef**
1 **tablespoon finely chopped scallions**
1 **egg, beaten**
1 **teaspoon salt**
1 **tablespoon soy sauce**
1 **tablespoon sugar**
1 **teaspoon sesame oil (optional)**
1 **tablespoon water**
1 **package wonton skins (use half a package, or about 65 skins)***
3 **cups vegetable oil (for deep frying) or**
2½ **15-ounce cans (about 5 cups) chicken or other broth (for soup)**

1. Mix all ingredients except wonton skins and oil or broth.

2. Put one teaspoon of mixture in the center of a wonton skin.

3. Moisten edges of skin with water and fold to form a triangle. Press edges together to seal.

4. Fill and fold rest of skins.

5. **To cook as appetizers:** Fry in hot oil until golden brown and crispy. (It is best to ask an experienced cook to help you with the deep frying.) Drain on a paper towel and serve hot with duck sauce (see page 12).

6. **To cook for use in soup:** Bring a large kettle of water to a boil. Add a few wonton at a time. Do not overcrowd; give them room to "swim" freely. Cook over medium heat for 8 to 10 minutes. Add cooked wonton to hot chicken broth or other soup base. Use about 3 dozen wonton to 5 cups of broth.

Makes 65 wonton

*Ready-made wonton skins, or noodles, can be found at many supermarkets and keep for several days in the refrigerator. If you freeze them, be sure to thaw them thoroughly before using.

Fried wonton are crisp, golden treats that are ideal appetizers and snacks.

Chicken and crunchy water chestnuts make egg-flower chicken soup a tasty first or main course. Top the soup with chopped green scallions.

SOUP

Soup is an important part of most Chinese meals. Generally, a light, clear soup is served as a drink between courses or throughout a meal. In a formal dinner, several kinds of thicker, richer soups may be served as courses in themselves. Soup is usually served in a big bowl in the middle of the table so that you can help yourself.

Egg-Flower Chicken Soup

½ cup raw chicken, cut into small pieces
1 tablespoon cornstarch
1 cup water
1 cup canned chicken broth
¼ cup thinly sliced water chestnuts
1 egg, beaten
1 tablespoon chopped scallions or
    parsley

1. In a small bowl, mix chicken pieces and cornstarch.
2. In a deep saucepan, bring water, chicken broth, and water chestnuts to a boil.
3. Add chicken mixture and bring back to a boil for about 10 minutes.
4. Stir in egg.
5. Sprinkle scallions or parsley on top.

Serves 4

Watercress Soup

½ cup lean raw pork, cut into small
    pieces
1 tablespoon soy sauce
1 tablespoon cornstarch
1 cup canned beef broth
1 cup water
1 bunch watercress, chopped, or
    2 cups any chopped leafy green
    vegetable such as Chinese
    cabbage, spinach, or chard

1. In a bowl, mix soy sauce and cornstarch. Add pork. Let stand for 15 minutes.
2. In a deep saucepan, bring beef broth and water to a boil.
3. Add pork. Cook over medium heat for 10 minutes.
4. Add watercress or other vegetable and cook uncovered for 2 minutes.

Serves 4

MAIN DISHES

A Chinese meal usually consists of several dishes, each of equal importance to the menu. Many of these dishes are combinations of meat or fish and vegetables and thus can be well-balanced meals alone. But usually several dishes are eaten together. Each of the recipes in this section feeds four people if served in combination with one or two other complementary dishes.

Fried Rice with Ham

Making fried rice is an excellent way to use odds and ends from the refrigerator. Fried rice is very economical, and it can be a complete and nourishing meal by itself. Different kinds of cooked meats and vegetables may be cut in small pieces and used to make various kinds of fried rice.

In the recipe below, you may substitute leftover roast beef, chicken, pork, turkey, Canadian bacon, or ordinary fried bacon. Cooked vegetables (about 1 cup) such as green beans, sugar peas, chopped cabbage, or bamboo shoots may be added to the rice as well.

4 cups cooked long-grain rice, cold (see page 21)
3 tablespoons vegetable oil
½ cup chopped onion
1 cup cooked ham, cut into small pieces
2 eggs, beaten
2 tablespoons soy sauce

1. Loosen and separate grains of rice.
2. Place a large skillet or wok over high heat. Add 2 tablespoons oil and heat thoroughly.
3. Fry onion to a light golden brown.
4. Add ham. Cook for 2 minutes, stirring constantly. Remove to a plate.
5. Add remaining 1 tablespoon oil to the skillet. Put in eggs and stir-fry until done.
6. Add rice to eggs. Stir in soy sauce. Put in ham and onion, mix thoroughly, and continue heating until completely hot.

Serves 4

White rice is especially good when fried with an egg and mixed with soy sauce, ham, bamboo shoots, and sliced mushrooms.

Stir-fried beef with sugar peas combines meat and crisp vegetables in a flavorful marinade.

Stir-Fried Beef with Sugar Peas

In making all stir-fried dishes, remember to work quickly. Have everything cut and measured before you start cooking. Cook the meat and vegetables just until they are tender.

If you cannot find sugar peas, use broccoli, green beans, or any other chopped green vegetable. Pork or chicken may also be used instead of beef.

1 pound flank steak
1 tablespoon soy sauce
1 tablespoon oyster sauce (optional)
2 tablespoons cornstarch
1 teaspoon sesame oil (optional)
1 teaspoon sugar
2 cups sugar peas
4 tablespoons vegetable oil
½ teaspoon salt
½ cup water chestnuts or bamboo shoots
½ cup sliced mushrooms

1. Cut beef across the grain into thin slices. (Meat is easier to cut thinly when it is partly frozen.)
2. Marinate beef in mixture of soy sauce, oyster sauce, cornstarch, sesame oil, and sugar. Set aside.
3. Remove stems and strings from sugar peas, leaving pods intact. Rinse and pat dry with paper towels.
4. Put 2 tablespoons vegetable oil in a hot skillet or wok. Add salt, sugar peas, water chestnuts, and mushrooms. Cook, stirring constantly, until peas become a darker green (about 2 minutes). Remove to a bowl.
5. In the same skillet, add remaining 2 tablespoons vegetable oil.
6. Add beef mixture and stir constantly until beef is almost done (5 minutes).
7. Return sugar peas, water chestnuts, and mushrooms to the skillet and mix thoroughly.

Serves 4

Tiny Cantonese-style barbequed spareribs can be served for an appetizer or as a main dish. They are marinated in several sauces, flavored with garlic and ginger, and brushed with honey.

Cantonese-Style Barbecued Spareribs

The ribs for this dish should be cut lengthwise across the bone before they are cooked. Ask your butcher to cut them for you.

2 pounds pork spareribs, cut apart
1 tablespoon minced fresh ginger root
1 tablespoon minced garlic
¼ cup soy sauce
¼ to ½ cup hoisin sauce
1 cup water
2 tablespoons honey

1. Mix all ingredients except water and honey. (Amount of hoisin sauce you use should depend on how salty you like your spareribs. Use only ¼ cup of hoisin sauce for a less salty marinating mixture.) Marinate spareribs in mixture for a few hours up to overnight.
2. Preheat the oven to 325°.
3. Put ribs on a rack in a roasting pan. (Save marinating mixture.) Pour water into the bottom of the pan.
4. Bake in the oven for 30 minutes.
5. Remove the pan from the oven and brush ribs on both sides with marinating mixture. Turn ribs over on the rack and return the pan to the oven for another 30 minutes.
6. Again remove from the oven and brush both sides of ribs with honey. Return to the oven for 10 more minutes.

Serves 4

Pork with green pepper and pineapple is a combination of meat, fruit, and vegetables in a sweet and sour sauce.

Pork with Green Pepper and Pineapple

This simple version of sweet and sour pork can be made with any lean cut of pork.

1 pound pork
2 tablespoons soy sauce
2 tablespoons cornstarch
1 tablespoon sugar
½ cup pineapple juice (drained from can of pineapple chunks)
3 tablespoons vegetable oil
1 cup ½-inch green pepper pieces
½ cup thinly sliced carrots
1 cup pineapple chunks

1. Slice pork thinly. (This is easiest when meat is partly frozen.)
2. Combine soy sauce and 1 tablespoon cornstarch in a bowl. Marinate pork in this mixture and set aside.
3. Mix remaining cornstarch with sugar and ½ cup pineapple juice. Set aside.
4. Heat oil in a large skillet or wok.
5. Add pork to the skillet and stir-fry until done.
6. Add pineapple juice mixture to meat and blend thoroughly. Set aside.
7. Stir-fry green pepper, carrots, and pineapple chunks for about 3 minutes. Blend thoroughly with other ingredients.

Serves 4

Carrots and green pepper lend a crunchy texture, and soy sauce adds flavor to pork with green pepper and pineapple.

Spiced Roast Chicken

a 3- to 4-pound roasting or frying chicken
¼ cup soy sauce
2 cloves garlic, crushed
1 teaspoon pepper
¼ cup sugar
2 tablespoons vegetable oil
several lettuce leaves

1. Rinse chicken in cool water and pat dry with paper towels.
2. Mix soy sauce, garlic, pepper, sugar, and oil in a bowl.
3. Thoroughly rub the inside and outside of chicken with this mixture.
4. Let chicken stand for 2 to 4 hours in the refrigerator.
5. Place chicken on a rack in a roasting pan and roast for 1½ hours at 350°. Turn chicken and brush with remaining soy sauce mixture every half hour during roasting.
6. When chicken is tender, remove from the oven. Cut into sections and arrange on a bed of lettuce on a serving platter.

Serves 4

Savory Beef Stew

This tender stewed meat can be served as a hot main dish for dinner. When cold, it can be thinly sliced to eat in sandwiches or as an appetizer.

1 tablespoon vegetable oil
1 clove garlic, crushed
1 slice fresh ginger root, minced
1 pound boned beef (rump roast or other similar cut)
½ cup soy sauce
1 cup canned beef broth
2 tablespoons sugar

1. Place a deep, heavy pot over high heat and add oil, garlic, and ginger root. Allow oil to heat until sizzling.
2. Place beef in the pot and brown it quickly on both sides.
3. Add remaining ingredients and bring to a boil.
4. Cover and turn down heat. Simmer for about 2 hours or until beef is tender.
5. Slice meat and serve with sauce in which it was cooked.

Serves 4

Shrimp with Hoisin Sauce

As a substitute for ½ cup of hoisin sauce, mix ¼ cup of Worcestershire sauce with ¼ cup of ketchup.

**1 pound medium-sized fresh shrimp
   in shells
½ cup water
1 tablespoon cornstarch
2 tablespoons soy sauce
½ cup hoisin sauce
¼ cup vegetable oil
2 slices fresh ginger root, minced
1 clove garlic, crushed
3 scallions, cut into 1-inch pieces**

1. Remove shells from shrimp. Split each shrimp down the back with a small knife and pull out the black or white vein. Rinse shrimp and dry on paper towels.
2. Mix water, cornstarch, soy sauce, and hoisin sauce in a bowl. Put aside.
3. Heat oil in a skillet or wok.
4. Add ginger root and garlic.
5. Add shrimp and stir until they change to a pink color (about 5 minutes).
6. Add scallions and stir-fry for 1 minute.
7. Add sauce mixture and cook for 2 minutes.

Serves 4

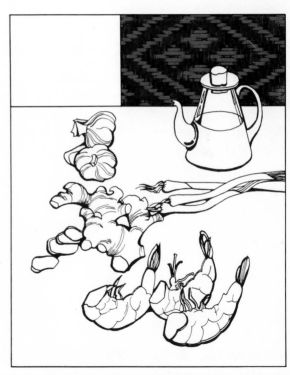

Ingredients for shrimp with hoisin sauce include shrimp, garlic, ginger root, and soy sauce.

Fresh vegetables are an important ingredient in Chinese cooking. They are cooked quickly to keep their original color, texture, and nutritional value.

VEGETABLES

Today, many supermarkets carry a limited variety of Chinese vegetables, including sugar peas (snow peas), bean sprouts, and Chinese (celery) cabbage. The most common American vegetables are adaptable to Chinese cooking, too.

Vegetables can be cooked by themselves or combined with other ingredients. In most cases, the cooking time for vegetables is short so the original color is retained and the texture remains crisp. Vitamins are not lost in this cooking method.

Chinese Cabbage

1 pound Chinese cabbage
½ cup canned chicken broth
1 tablespoon cornstarch
2 tablespoons vegetable oil
1 teaspoon salt

1. Wash cabbage and dry with paper towels. Cut into 1-inch pieces.

2. Mix chicken broth and cornstarch. Put aside.
3. Heat oil in a skillet or wok.
4. Add Chinese cabbage and salt. Stir-fry for 4 minutes.
5. Add cornstarch mixture and mix all ingredients well.

Serves 4

Bean Sprouts with Scallions

2 tablespoons vegetable oil
1 19-ounce can bean sprouts, drained, or 1 pound fresh bean sprouts
1 teaspoon salt
4 scallions, cut into 1-inch pieces

1. Heat oil in a skillet or wok.
2. Add bean sprouts. Stir-fry for 2 minutes. Add salt.
3. Stir in scallions and cook for 2 more minutes.

Serves 4

DESSERTS

The Chinese eat very few desserts. Usually they end a meal with fresh fruit. Pastries and sweet dishes *are* made in China, but they are special festival foods and are rarely served with the daily meal.

In the West, people often end a Chinese meal with fortune cookies. Like chop suey, however, these cookies are unknown in China. A recipe for fortune cookies has been included in this book because they are so much fun to make and eat. Just remember that the first two recipes in this section provide a more authentic choice of Chinese sweets.

Almond Fruit Float

Any kind of fruit, fresh or canned, may be used in this recipe. Mandarin oranges, sliced peaches, fruit cocktail, and pineapple make delicious floats.

1 envelope unflavored gelatin
1 cup water
½ cup sugar

½ cup milk
1 tablespoon almond extract
1 13-ounce can fruit with syrup

1. In a saucepan, dissolve gelatin in water. Place over high heat and bring to a boil. Then reduce heat to low.
2. Add sugar and stir until thoroughly dissolved.
3. Stir in milk and almond extract. Mix well.
4. Pour into a deep, square pan and allow to set at room temperature. Then put in refrigerator to cool.
5. When cool, cut into cubes and serve topped with fruit and syrup. (If there is not enough syrup with the fruit, make a syrup by mixing 1 cup of water with 3 tablespoons sugar and ¼ teaspoon almond extract. Chill and serve with fruit and gelatin.)

Serves 6

Almond fruit float, a refreshing dessert that goes especially well with almond cookies or fortune cookies (recipes on page 40), can be made with either fresh or canned fruit.

Almond Cookies

2½ cups all-purpose flour
1 cup sugar
1 teaspoon baking soda
¼ teaspoon salt
1 cup vegetable shortening
2 eggs, beaten
1 tablespoon almond extract
¼ cup blanched unsalted almonds

1. Mix dry ingredients in a bowl.
2. Cut shortening into dry ingredients with a fork or pastry cutter.
3. Add beaten eggs and almond extract. Stir with a spoon until well mixed.
4. Preheat the oven to 325°.
5. Shape dough into balls the size of a large cherry.
6. Put on greased cookie sheets. Press an almond down in the center of each cookie.
7. Bake for 25 minutes.

Makes about 4 dozen cookies

Fortune Cookies

To make fortunes, cut white paper into 25 strips about 2 inches long and ¾ inch wide and write a fortune on each one.

1 cup margarine, softened
½ cup sugar
1 egg
2½ teaspoons vanilla extract
3¼ cups flour
½ teaspoon baking powder

1. Mix together margarine, sugar, and egg until smooth. Then add other ingredients. Mix everything together to form a ball of dough.
2. Lightly flour a wooden board or flat surface. With a rolling pin, roll half of dough very thin. Use a circle-shaped cookie cutter or the top of a large glass (about 2½ inches wide) to cut out circles in dough. (You may cut dough in other shapes, if you wish.)
3. Put a fortune in each circle, off to one side. Fold the circle in half and then in half again. Pinch it to close.

4. Preheat the oven to 425°.

5. Reroll cut scraps of dough and make cookies from them. Then roll and make cookies from other half of dough.

6. Bake cookies for about 10 minutes or until they are lightly browned. Serve when cool.

Makes 25 cookies

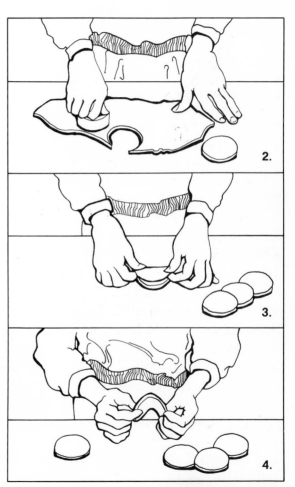

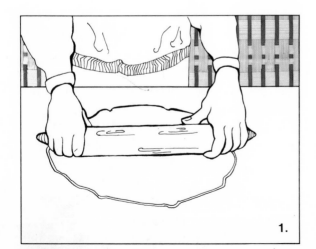

Left: **Roll the dough very thin.** *Right:* **Cut out the cookies, fold each one over, and fold each in half again.**

THE CAREFUL COOK

Whenever you cook, there are certain safety rules you must always keep in mind. Even experienced cooks follow these rules when they are in the kitchen.

1. Always wash your hands before handling food.
2. Thoroughly wash all raw vegetables and fruits to remove dirt, chemicals, and insecticides.
3. Use a cutting board when cutting up vegetables and fruits. Don't cut them up in your hand! And be sure to cut in a direction *away* from you and your fingers.
4. Long hair or loose clothing can easily catch fire if brought near the burners of a stove. If you have long hair, tie it back before you start cooking.
5. Turn all pot handles toward the back of the stove so that you will not catch your sleeves or jewelry on them. This is especially important when younger brothers and sisters are around. They could easily knock off a pot and get burned.

6. Always use a pot holder to steady hot pots or to take pans out of the oven. Don't use a wet cloth on a hot pan because the steam it produces could burn you.
7. Lift the lid of a steaming pot with the opening away from you so that you will not get burned.
8. If you get burned, hold the burn under cold running water. Do not put grease or butter on it. Cold water helps to take the heat out, but grease or butter will only keep it in.
9. If grease or cooking oil catches fire, throw baking soda or salt at the bottom of the flame to put it out. (Water will *not* put out a grease fire.) Call for help, and try to turn all the stove burners to "off."

METRIC CONVERSION CHART

WHEN YOU KNOW		MULTIPLY BY	TO FIND	
MASS (weight)				
ounces	(oz)	28.0	grams	(g)
pounds	(lb)	0.45	kilograms	(kg)
VOLUME				
teaspoons	(tsp)	5.0	milliliters	(ml)
tablespoons	(Tbsp)	15.0	milliliters	
fluid ounces	(oz)	30.0	milliliters	
cup	(c)	0.24	liters	(l)
pint	(pt)	0.47	liters	
quart	(qt)	0.95	liters	
gallon	(gal)	3.8	liters	
TEMPERATURE				
Fahrenheit	(°F)	5/9 (after	Celsius	(°C)
temperature		subtracting 32)	temperature	

COMMON MEASURES AND THEIR EQUIVALENTS

3 teaspoons = 1 tablespoon

8 tablespoons = ½ cup

2 cups = 1 pint

2 pints = 1 quart

4 quarts = 1 gallon

16 ounces = 1 pound

1. Tea
2. Wonton
3. Spiced Roast Chicken
4. Watercress Soup
5. Fried Rice with Ham
6. Savory Beef Stew
7. Stir-Fried Beef with Sugar Peas
8. Bean Sprouts with Scallions
9. Chinese Cabbage
10. Pork with Green Pepper
    and Pineapple
11. Shrimp with Hoisin Sauce
12. Almond Fruit Float
13. Rice
14. Egg-Flower Chicken Soup
15. Cantonese-Style
    Barbequed Spareribs
16. Almond Cookies
17. Fortune Cookies

4. 西洋菜湯

5. 火腿炒飯

6. 紅燒牛肉

7. 雪豆牛肉

8. 炒豆芽

9. 炒白菜

10. 青椒豬肉

11. 海鮮蝦仁

12. 杏仁豆腐

13. 白飯

1. 茶

2. 餛飩

3. 焗雞

Chinese characters by Ling Yu

14.

15.

雞肉蛋花湯

廣東烤排骨

16.

17.

杏仁餅

簽語餅

INDEX

ABOUT THE AUTHOR

Ling Yu was born in Nanjing (Nanking), China. Before coming to the United States, she attended Providence College in Taiwan. Later she graduated from the University of Dayton (Ohio) with a major in home economics and a library science minor.

Since 1970, Yu has been Audiovisual Librarian at the Reading Public Library in Reading, Pennsylvania. Prior to that, she worked at the library on the main campus of Pennsylvania State University. Yu is also a freelance translator for publishers in Taiwan, specializing in the areas of child development and publishing.

For a number of years, Yu has been teaching various courses and giving demonstrations in Chinese cooking. She also returns frequently to Taiwan to visit and to learn more about Chinese cuisine.

easy menu
ethnic
cookbooks

Cooking the **CHINESE** Way
Cooking the **ENGLISH** Way
Cooking the **FRENCH** Way
Cooking the **ITALIAN** Way
Cooking the **JAPANESE** Way
Cooking the **MEXICAN** Way
Cooking the **NORWEGIAN** Way
Cooking the **SPANISH** Way

Lerner Publications Company
241 First Avenue North, Minneapolis, Minnesota 55401

ACKNOWLEDGMENTS: The illustrations are reproduced through the courtesy of; pp. 2, 18, 20, 30, 32, 39, Robert L. Wolfe; pp. 4, 23, California Olive Industry; pp. 24, 36, 48, Burch Communications, Inc.; p. 27, CHUN KING® Oriental Foods, a product of Del Monte Corporation (left), Rice Council of America (right); p. 28, La Choy Food Products. Cover photograph by Robert L. Wolfe.